The Four Sufferings

Shiku hakku

poetry

TERRY WATADA

MAWEN*Z*I
HOUSE

We acknowledge the support of the Canada Council for the Arts for our publishing program. We also acknowledge support from the Government of Ontario through the Ontario Arts Council, and the support of the Government of Canada through the Canada Book Fund.

Cover design by Sabrina Pignataro
Cover photo: YasushigeMaruo / Colored maple leaves stock photo / iStockphoto
Author photo credit: Tane Akamatsu

Library and Archives Canada Cataloguing in Publication

Title: The four sufferings : shiku hakku : poetry / Terry Watada.
Names: Watada, Terry, 1951- author.
Identifiers: Canadiana (print) 20200310704 | Canadiana (ebook) 20200310720 | ISBN 9781774150177
   (softcover) | ISBN 9781774150184 (EPUB) | ISBN 9781774150191 (PDF)
Classification: LCC PS8595.A79 F68 2020 | DDC C811/.54—dc23

Printed and bound in Canada by Coach House Printing

Mawenzi House Publishers Ltd.
39 Woburn Avenue (B)
Toronto, Ontario M5M 1K5
Canada
www.mawenzihouse.com

Contents

Shiku Hakku

In contemporary Japan, *shiku hakku* means to endure hardship or to suffer as in "I *shiku hakku* to pass my exams". The expression's origins lie in Buddhism. I grew up in the Toronto Buddhist Church and always heard the expression, "Life is *dukkha*". "Life is suffering"—the first of the Four Noble Truths. Little did I know it contained a little more detail and a deeper meaning.

Dukkha contains four basic sufferings [*shiku*] that must be endured by all human beings: birth, aging, illness and death. Add to that four additional sufferings [*hakku*]: the pain of separation; the pain of suffering fools; the pain of desire; and the overall pain and suffering of existence.

So it was I came to write the poems of *The Four Sufferings*. The collection links my past to my present state of existence. And though some may consider the poems dark, sombre, perhaps grim, I see them as an honest celebration of all those I've known: those I've suffered and those I've loved. In the end, I seek the enlightened state of acceptance. Rise above life's hardships and rejoice in the state of life.

I was not born a Buddhist. Furthermore, I wasn't born Shinto, Christian, Muslim, Sikh, or Hindu. I came from nothing; I wasn't anything, but I do try to live as a Buddhist. Perhaps this allows me to deal with the above *yojijukugo* (a four-character idiom). My degree of success lies imbedded in the poetry.

In the Valley of the Temples

the *Byodo-in*
        grace-
    fully beams   with

the   Buddha's
serenity,   compassion
and
      dharma

an "abode of
light
      and love"
as Iwamura *sensei*
would have said.

and there are stands of bamboo
surrounding;   the wise
     & sturdy
   stems
        grow into
   the sky   taking root
   in the   blue
   and cloud

but
     their stalks are
    scarred

by proclamations
of
    love & fidelity

by tourists and locals

they
        deface   like
12-year-olds

a *haole*   more
comfortable
with a   bottle of beer,
        baseball cap
and television set
gouges
                mindlessly,
professing   his
love for his dim-
witted
girlfriend   (observing.

Of course, the gesture
touches her moisture   if not
her watery
        sentimental
    eyes.

the two stand   dumb
and   blind
in the glow
        of infinite
    light

the bamboo   complain
with
        creaks, pops, clicks
    and clacks
    as the knives dig deeper

their suffering scars
my own heart . . .
but they do not fall.

I soon realize   they
do
        not ache because
    of inconsequential vanity

the creaks are of age   the pops
fractured
            limbs
    the clicks   photos

of lost friends   the cracks
of loneliness
and
        perhaps despair.

But they never fall.

such is my gratitude
for the
        Buddha.

in gassho

Kaneohe, Hawaii

ONE

the irony   of rain
is that
        it never ends

it's always raining   some-
where—
            rain:
      the giver of life.

in the storm of birth.

here's that rainy day

a chevron of   strings
a sad
        ballad   (a stream of
air in perfect   harmony)

calls
for the rain to come

with
        warm, blue & black
clouds   high
above
                and
    low to the ground

a calm settles
until   a fine mist
flourishes
                and coats the day
    with the promise of
    the new.

but I sit before the dark & clear bay window
listening
                to vinyl from a tube
amp   sonic comfort   while watching
droplets painting the glass   pointillist
images   emerging
with fog varnishing my eyes

as
if to sing   *here's that rainy*
day by jimmy van heusen & johnny burke

content to wait
out the rolling thunder
and
gathering storm.

[playing witness to the beginning of life]

Osaka Airs

Osaka
        airs
                burn
on   brilliantly
the stairs   in the crisp light
        of Shimbashi
Station   he lies   like an *inemuri*

flat   still and stiff
        as if inviting every/anyone
      to walk the   plank

his shoes are
rough,   broken and
battered with his journey
through
            life,
      his clothes   dirty
      and smudged with
      insult and spit

his hair smeared
with
congealed shit and
dust mites   his only
companions   the

aroma of
    3-day sweat, urine
stains   and
the indignities
of
    inherited poverty,

but it is his face
that's
    frightening:

petrified
   and scarred by
street concrete   and
em-
    barr
   assment

can't tell if he is breathing
no
    one stops
  to find out   to stop and care

he lies stiff with each tripod step
holding   him up;
corpse-like lying in state

in distant Osaka

the wind circles
the   streets
and
        slices off
        gingko leaves,

the leaves swirl
within
a golden cyclone
        and
flow through-
                out the
        south

the airs link and
fly from
                kansai
        to kanto

slip and
        slither
        down a sub-

way opening   [like a miyazaki
        dragon]
until the
                shards of
        gold

cover & adhere to him

coating
him with a gold-
leaf   skin
he glows anew   a rebirth
in a city's rush

attracting a rush-hour
crowd
and we gather during the
visitation   for a   saint.

the patron saint of the homeless
and the reborn

Osaka airs
moan
        and groan
    forcing us
        to bow in reverential supplication.

Cloudburst

a
        Toronto summer-
    storm
            is like
    no other:

humidity   gathers, piles
up
        into a pregnant mass   which   swells
bigger   and higher and higher
as each trimester passes,

until it squeezes against   the thunderhead,
until
        lightning cracks
and punctures the   clouddeck

a cloud-   burst
    water-
falls
            upon
        the city

below.

i sit in the empty
100-year-old
and
        still bedroom
in awe,

watching rivers
and streams   sweeping
twigs,
            autumnal leaves,
and streetgarbage   to the
sewer
            mouths,
voracious like starving
feral dogs,

gobbling the effluent deluge
of civilization

the cloying
                smell
  of humidity
  rises
            from the
asphalt and
lawns,
            seeping through the
window frame:
a reminder of the grave

i look   through
the
        cloud-
burst to the blue

and beg a return
to
        foreign lands,
un-intelligible tongues,

oshogatsu

food, warm
     comfortable
   flavours

the perfume of her motherly hair
and the touch of her mother's palms,

hoping
the rain will stop soon
and bring the promise
of clear,
        blue skies

At the Bottom of the Stairs

my
     son
  is twenty-one
  years old

but i
     recall the sound
  of his long fall
          down
  the stairs

go-ro go-ro go-ro   stop
go-ro go-ro go-ro   stop
an aching   (pause) before
     the shrill call   of
   his crying

there   i
found *okaa* & child   sitting
on the second   step   at
the bottom
       of the
     stairs

  a set that creaked at the
  13th step,
  a set that is in a house
  that is 100 years old

  bottomstairs   where
  my mother's water broke
  and I slid into the world]

her arms wrapped
around
            her babychild,
soothing love
and safety;

  he wailing   and then
  sniffling & hiccupping

more shock than pain

dombura kokko sukkokko
the sound
        of a peach boy rolling
    tumbling
                    down
a riverslide until an aged
couple stopped   it
and rejoiced at the end
of their hunger

a baby emerged
        like any child
from its   aromatic,
sweet amniotic fluid

and the couple were overjoyed.

like my father and mother, like my wife
and me.

the onomatopoeic sound of love
in
      Japan
      and home.

Reflections in a turquoise-blue Swimming Pool

a plumeria
    blossom
  floats on deep turquoise
  water
     its petals
soft,
  brilliant-white, full of pain &
 supple above the inviting

primordial bath

as bunji-baby
rests his foot within the opening
tenderness of birth

to take his first step,
he
   looks up
 and smiles as the world celebrates

the baby Buddha

His smile comprises the
width of existence and
the breadth of choral,
angelic
    voices]

*

Up   above,
the
      surrounding trees   on display
      festooned with a galaxy of flowers

a crown of plumeria
ring-
      -ing   encircling
  the eternal

    black
    with lightning-bug stars
    faint, perhaps fading   but
    most assuredly there

all babies
      come
   forward   enlightened

& leave
with traces of hope
in
      their absence

for my son, naturally
Honolulu

The Horizon

as I scan the land-
        scape
of
      jazz tracks, heat distortions and
black-
        clumps
  of Japanese   in Shibuya

far beneath
       the Starbuck chaos
  and outside the Seibu
  air-   conditioned
        civility,

my son and wife come into focus
for a moment
at
      the delta of the scramble
  cross-walk

they smile
   while withering
   in the august-heat
beating   of the summer drum
that drones of   *buy and sell*

but I see the horizon
of sun   rise
and
    set
and reach out for their embrace

Tokyo, Japan

II.

The Crooked Buddha

Namu amida butsu
Namu amida butsu
Namu amida butsu

he
        stands
crooked in his
infirmities   leaning
on   2 canes

his *koshi* curved   to
the sun   his
balding   head burnished
red
            the sparse *kami*
no ke   turned faces away
turned heels away
from   hair, paper,
and gods

the *sutra*   spews
forth
        from withered lips
    his decaying *kuchi*
        perfumed with   death

bloodless hands   and
stick-figure legs   wobble

each & every   morning
he
         hobbles from his lair

   a hidden Buddhist temple
   in yotsuya, Tokyo,

and yes, the crooked Buddha
chants   every morning

not for himself, but for all who
pass by   without
gratitude.
    without enlighten-
ment.

namu amida butsu
namu amida butsu
namu amida butsu

The City: *the young shall inherit*

It's a smoke-ring
afternoon
            with   the skyline
    chimneys   cough-ing

up
        their corporate
    commerce.

the street   rivers
(greasy with slime &
    rainwater)
    are
        choked with
        mobs and machines

the choir of the city
climbs
            the vertical vertebrae
to
        coat the cataract windows with

the 21st century.

all the neophyte, emerging and [frank &
earnest]
            dilettante
        poets

begin   with
            midnight

wanderings downtown
below   the attacking   neon

calling, enticing,   lying, cheating, conning
and
          twisted party-boys, negro gangsters
          oriental hipsters and video whores
          no more or less
                than their tattoos,
                      muscle-shirts, short-skirts
          bare legs, brass knuckles and spiked heels   hanging out.

neighbourhood colonies:
C   hina-town [with narrowing
alleys leading into
darkness]

Little
          italy, india
     greektown   korea-
     town

[phosphorescent burning lights
     throbbing with pain]
     offering
                food (kalbi, ro-tini,
          biryani . . . spanakopita
) for   cash

malvern
          janefinch
danzig street under twisted neon
sign[s

glaring eyes turned yellow
in the dark]

the barren Sudantown   glistens
in the sallow streetlights
of a Syrian   delusion
and police tape

while
        would-be
    artists, poets and musicians

find inspiration in
the garbage- filled
shit-smeared   roads
to
        murder-poverty

I hear the singer singin' his songs
in
        the skank bars   the city

morgues
                tryin'
    to make sense of the abbreviated
    and distorted   word

like tryin' to understand
the Holy Trinity: Buddha-jesus, lennon & Dylan
so, he sings:

"They say I'm old but
                    they
        ain't getting any younger."

I hear you, brother.

I sit
        in the
    mottled light of a metropolis
    streaming into an obsolete, antiquated, archaic
    cathedral   from above

antediluvian for the modern;
I realize
        I am tired,
        just tired.

it is the longest
day   in a short life
and the young buddha-
heads

bray
        and whine
    like a president of the disjointed
    states

but I can no longer
listen;
        all I can do is close
my eyes
        and think on
    the absurdity of the
    man on the cross

before gazing up at the shining city
upon the hill
and
    falling asleep.

When the *Issei* Danced

when
          the *Issei*   danced
      it was a time of cele-
      bration

a thing of joy

at hideki's wedding,
taka-
          hashi-*san*
tied his necktie
around his   head   an improvised *hachimaki*
with fan
              in hand
jumped   to his feet
and
          cavorted to an
    ancient   *minyo*

he contorted his face
in
            every which way
lips one way, his eyes
the other

he kicked his crooked
leg   up to the res-
taurant dining-room ceiling   while

twirling
    the fan
with his fingers
in geometric patterns

his hands   in choreographed
positions

the children giggled   everyone
else laughed
especially *Okaasan*

Father smiled.
at grandpa's 88th birthday—

Beiju

    while rikimatsu, tohana
    and kawai-*san*   raised glasses
    of Johnny Walker Red   (going
    all out for this one)
    before the banquet of Chinese
    cuisine on teetering tables

fujiwara-*san*
        smacked
his hands together
announcing
a
celebration   an *odori*, a dance, dance, dance

and everyone clapped in time
as he sang
acapella   his voice soaring
to the ancestral spirits

and they sang back

tsuki-ga deta deta, tsuki-ga deta   oi yoi-yoi

the ethereal notes
wept   in the airconditioning
as
        grandpa stood to join-in
        and fujiwara-*san*
        danced
            like a young man

punctuated by grunts and
calls to join in   they floated
on   the notes of an old
        folk song—

the   melody   of
    community.

a 50th wedding anniversary
in the basement of   *China
House*
            when dad kissed
        mom—a fisherman's daughter

for the first time to my
recollection

and cheers rose like disturbed
dust
        and the white-jacket
waiters served the abalone
in rich brown sauce

(a taste of the BC coast)
their home three decades
ago

and they held hands
while a gang
      of *issei* circled around
  them

the blessed couple smiled
in happiness.

their two sons   shed
the blood
      of memory
& voices rose in song:

Yaren soran soran soran soran.
Hai hai.

A dokkoisho dokkoisho.

*

when the *issei* danced
to the rhythms
          of old Japan
     they pantomimed
     the lyrics

and memories cried—
a sight to behold   of love unfold-
ing

chan-to, chan-to, chan-to

Walking down the boulevard,
with the hairdo of a married woman . . .

I'm a wisteria hanging above,
and you're a lily below.

it is amusing   but all
disappears when
I
     awake to the   lonely, cold
     clarity.   of morn-   ing.

The Longest Night of the Year

December
      with its frozen
sleep
and grey-fabric days

the month contains
the longest night
of the   year.

But   there come the
count-
        less   dinners
   in intimate candlelight

in the raw/scrapped
glare
     of cafeterias
in the bare-bulb'd kitchens
of home
        in the
unflattering fluorescence
of
     diners   the muted

   sadness   of local
   cafés

inside
      the shadow'd   corners
of gluttonous buffets

in-side   the elegance of the formal
ban-
          quet
and in the formality of
haute cuisine
are the bits of light that warm

that
keep you company   even in
iso-la-tion

they built a wall in China
to keep
the infidels away
they
          built
  a wall in Berlin

to keep the east within;

they built
a
          wall in the holyland
  to keep enemies apart

they want
a wall
          along
      the border
to keep the immigrants
at
      bay

and I want a
wall
      around me
    forsaking friends
    and family

to keep the toxins in check
and the brightlight inside.

and yet the
cold
      winds   invisible in
the black air
mask
the   light
during the longest night

four
      in
    the morning

mourning   the long-
lost day   and the singers
sing
a   poetic melody

in a layered
      choir of
music
into
      my ear
like rain on a drum

down

        through

   my ages

Deep Purple

when
　　　the
deep purple falls . . .

the luxurious　tempo
of
the song　with touches of

nostalgia
　　　　and light
(thick music　warm & familiar)
　gives me
　　　　comfort.

april sings　to me
in　a
　　low
　sweet voice

conjures up
old
　　　girlfriends
　longago girls

I only　see them
while I sleep:
tickles of long hair
as I gaze at the promise
of
　　touch and dew

but I awake in
   candlelight
  shadows

before the hearth
of
  empty fire
and think of love
as
  an adolescent pursuit

i have to smile as
the music crescendos
   and sub-
  sides.

we'll always meet here
in my deep purple dreams

3.

by Starlight

the winter
       solstice
     stretched and pulled
     the night sky   to an inordinate
     length

and the music reached for
the great   photosphere
above

roy's still got
his chops   still chasing
evans;
        heavens
     bill evans

like some demon obsessed
kept   young
at the age of 90   to hit those
modalities   to improvise into
the darkness   of space and time

and *Stella*
comes to him
like
       the light of
   stars   weeping on

his shoulders

lingering smell of
isopropyl
    alcohol
in the seniors' home

reminds him of the hospital bed

where
    she
  lies

wraparound sunglasses
and
    bandaged legs

she remains incognito.

and when he hit the
chorus
    she's every-
  thing
      on Earth
    to me.

the   piano
    notes   chimed
  out   her eulogy

starlight   showered   &
coated his dream

and made it sparkle like a dark star.

for roy and holly

The Blues

"brother ray, he got
     a woman   way
    over town . . .

and so begins the blues

I.

"use to play sax
          for
    ray charles.

started down in New
Orleans, thru to Jackson, Mississippi:
the delta,
     where my people
are from;

up to Chicago, like robert
johnson . . .   but I wasn't poisoned.
don't drink from no bottle
I didn't open
my
     self.

ended up in
     new york
  city

that's how I got to here."

brother ray swings
in
    his bright darkness:

  the keys reflected in
  his glasses

as the blur of the blues
streams
      from his fingers

"now you take dem raelettes,
  they
     was fine   sweet as honey
  and easy to look at"

we sat
in
Sai Woo one Saturday
[old immigrant
      restaurant
when the only jobs available for
chinamen were in laundries &
restaurants   ]

Superior men, Humans, China   men

#4 with eggroll   special today

the squeal of metal tables and plastic
wear   absorbed the sadness in the kitchen

but 1970s *dim sum* when Nixon opened China:
scrumptious morsels
of pork and shrimp   nice crunch to them

we laughed and ate

Akira   was in town
from nyc   had a gig at the Senator

and he invited me along
to talkstory and eat food

the saxman   in his band
was
            tall, thin with
            a friendly face and
            cynical eyes

  he used to play horn with ray
  charles.   back in the day
  when
            he lived the blues
  when he was the blues

yes, we laughed the afternoon away
until
            the jazz and music consumed us
            at night.   like the fire in ray's
blind-
            genius

i clung to Akira as he drummed
through his solo   that night.

he was a good man   friendly man
generous man
i
    miss him in these
  bluedays of dark

skies and melodious wind.

"ray, shit, he never drank *pepsi*,
   just did it   for the money."

2.

sing sean, sing in that old rebel's voice:

well, you'll wonder where the yellow went
when you brush your teeth with pepsodent

you'll wonder
    where the yellow
  went . . .

I marvel at an angry young Chinese man singing
all   those
years ago   back in '72 when

the smoke   rose
    in the choked
attic air
of the House   on mutual street.

Our mutual stand; our
      mutual love for that which
is Asian and Canadian.

in the aromatic
and   narcotic smoke
when   sean

and martin
     jammed
to chris, joanne

and   'charlie'
    chan   chin   all
night   long

you'll wonder
    where the yellow
  went

where did the yellow go?

3.

and charlie sang,
played   those
        jazz
  chords

I marveled at his dexterity.

"hey man, you played with
  Hendrix, right?"

he nodded into a diminished new york 7th.

"he teach you anything?"

Don't trust no-one.

imagine   that,
stephen stills ripped off
the wandering
china-
        man.

we all got them
ol' yellowman blues.

sing dem old *Nikkei* blues: *we are the children of the migrant*
   worker . . .

4.

Le Coq D'or tavern
the
        place
     of r&blues & dreams

ronnie (a hair swept
german/jpze/cdn
             teen of guitar
chords and song)   and i
stood
out-side   bent warped axes
in hand staring at
posters and flyers
of
     old:

the fabulous Penguins,
all-star   atlantic record
review   *the Five Satins*
and the smooth Commodores

caught mid-performance

cool, cool, cool   and cool

the bouncer let us into
     an afternoon   jam show
with Willie Dixon

[the great blues
man from Chicago's
South
        Side.

he stood
before us like some   dark
Colossus

smiling like night,
his diamonds
            & teeth sparkling
like stars

and he made the fretboard sing
before
looking
            down
    at us and inviting

us on stage.

Ronnie balked but
I jumped at the chance.

Otis span tickled
the ivories   bernardo
dennis   cut
the guitar   and ol' bassman
Willie was the   foundation.

the count-down
and
        we ripped into

Everyday I have the Blues

Muddy waters, howlin' wolf,
junior wells
they was all with me

until a booming voice
called a halt to my glory.

I   looked at
mr. Dixon;   he scowled.

All he said was, "I think you'd better tune up, boy."

I crumbled and sought the middle-eight to disappear.

5.

Roy and butch
riffcd on   a tune
by
        roy
in the studio

two Jpze Cdns
with a   love of   jazz

who   never
played together
but played with
others

roy with phil nimmons
butch
with oscar Peterson

"never with ellington or basie . . .
Jammed with 'em tho."

Roy called me *The Kid*
and
        Butch advised,
    always date
    married   women

"No complaints, And they're so grateful."

I bet   Oscar wasn't.

6.

a west coast city
        a west coast
        Asian city

and deems, you remember deems?
yeah,
        that cool Seattle jazz cat
caressing the ivories   the 88s
in some
        bar between Chinatown
    and tomorrow morning

in the 1930s;
trying to make
                a living.
reminiscent of roy & butch,
ryo fukui

saw him again in Vancouver,
another west coast city
in the 90s,
another
        Asian
      city.

still playing,
       still trying
       to make a living.

not bad for a jap jazzman—

as he was promoted.

7.

akira   once introduced me to
jim hall
         a
mellow guitar swung thru
the music
at the
       club
   blue note

akira sat me in   front of
toshiko   akiyoshi
her
   jpze beauty danced
  across the keys like
  an *odori*

I fell in love.

akira   offered
to
        sit-in next   time
I recorded.

I turned red   and
thank-ed him   with   all
my soul and spirit

but he was too good
for the likes of me.

Too good.   bless him

*

all the friends, fellow musicians
loved
        ones [wife and
    child],

audience members sway around
my palliative   dream-bed
like the *Issei* once did for
my parents (
keeping me company as
memories spark &
sputter out   )

but
    come back to life
  in my rage

rage against the enveloping-closing night;
rage against
                the dying.

Forgive me, I pray,
[as I warp & distort the villanelle]

hey mr. d.j.!   keep
spinning 'em
platters and   let me
dance to the music   every-one
dance
        to the 'ol yellow man
    blues.

what choice we got?
warm beer and cold women
              Ol' Tom, that's
what
his life's been.

Ol' Whiskey and Whiskers.

And so ends the song, so predicts the end.

The Coffin of Night

when i
    wake up, the coffin of night
encloses   blinds me
chokes   me
        until i hear
my
    father scrapping along
    the linoleum

his Parkinsonian legs
stick him to the
floor
        as he struggles
  to understand   and crying
  out of ignorance

and as i bump and scratch
my own way   over the carpet and
through the   enclosures of
the hour

with the pain of arthritis & fracture

i wonder
        if my son is
    listening

and will his   in another
generation?

some—
        times i cry
    as
        my father did

because i
            know

what will   be.

Four

Ghost Sleep

my eyes
          are
     brittle

i can't
     move;
  i can only see

the backs of my
eye
     lids

i must be in
the deep
       sleep of
     ghosts

i'm caught in the
throat-choking   grasp
of   a
thick   west coast
mountain forest

and then i see him,
burning brightly   in
luminescent air,
taking
       great
  strides across
  the black landscape

his arms
      strong & vital
flailing   about his head
like
      some mystical spirit

during creation.

i see
      his confident
open-mouth'd   smile

i hear his laugh   like
he never   laughed
in life,
      not like that.

a grin across his
face   sharing the
joke, the   anecdote,
the moment
with   friends

but then I   see:
he's
      dragging
the wind behind him

[timber, branches and stumps swirl & tumble in his wake]

with the strength of gods
the
    compassion of the Buddha
  and the love of
  fam- ily

otouchan

he turned to me
and smiled.
       the dream
     dissolved into   drizzle

i awake   to a rainy day
and
     taste
  the moist gauze

of ghosts.

Poem inspired by my father's dream in his last days.

Standing in Fields of Wheat

I can see
            him
    standing amongst

the wheat   their shafts
un-
        dulating in the rollin'
    field   of birth

the wind   tousles
his shaggy hair
        playfully;
    he smiles   a

beatific, charming
smile

he must be 8,
maybe younger . . .   seems
just about   right

his shirt is rumpled
old . . . used   understated
plaid
his favourite thrown away
by an insensitive mother

years later   when
it was
        worn out;

the   coarse wool
pants ride high on his
waist   (rough crude material
darker
than the earth beneath his
scuffed brown shoes.

the pant legs
    are short with an
ambition to be called
shorts

a 1940s look   )
his body
is
    thin   due to a
lack   of
nutrition, lack of fresh fruit

but
he looks   happy
maybe he is,
even if   evacuated
(banished)   into exile

i never knew him to be happy.

the sea of wheat waved like the
pacific ocean   something
he
    yearned to hear, taste
  see,   late in life.

For my brother
I hope he was happy for a time.

A Man of Regret

the room   was full of
light
              brilliant, pure
   light   cascading
                  from
   the highabove sky-light,

and yellow sun droplets   stain
the gathered
who
      had come to say they
   were sorry   to demonstrate that
   they cared.

the minister   mustered
as much
              compassion
as his Buddha
nature   allowed

and no kinder words were said.

a child of the Depression,   hated in
the streets and school;
the kidnapping of his father in the night,
Internment [imprisoned by forest, isolation,
and self-hatred],
exiled   resettlement, hostility & prejudice,
. . . a sense of worthlessness.

a house
        in the suburbs, middle-class stifling,
& then isolation . . . estrangement from blood;
hope in a son.

friends & family cried
as soft
            as   glycerine rain

the corpse lay in its coffin
as peace   grew like moss
under-
            neath

a comfortable
            cushion
    against eternity

we sat in silence   mediating
on his life   and i remembered   his words
of regret:

i always wanted to go to Kyoto
to offer
        incense
    to the Buddha at

Kiyomizu-dera   to wait for
Kannon   to make her   appearance
in her 32nd year
            to revere

the   sword-sensei Masamune
to
         buy   his
work of art   (maybe
at a discount!)

[he chuckled to himself]   but
the gleam of the blade
is warm   to the touch

painless as it cuts
10,000   mongol   heads,
armour and helmets,
without   suffering a dent
in the molten kill of the blade

         such is legend

& such are his wishes:
to watch
my
grandchildren   so that
i
     may dance at their weddings

to kiss my granddaughter goodbye
until
         she becomes a mother

and welcome my great grandchild
to this unfathomable   ephemeral world.

and yet nothing of me,   no mention
of a brother whatsoever,   yet a memory
in the midst of clarity: he squeezed my hand

by his palliative-care-
bed
           and his eyes
welled-up   like saturated
earth
      the regret of
    lost brother-
    hood

of accusations   of snide remarks
to   humiliate
to shred
      into pieces—

the self becoming worthless—

for my sins,
for the years of his absence   for
his fearful presence   for
my parents loving me,
he called
           me "lucky"

but i hated you out of love   a
deathbed confession

the pools of his tears
are deep   yet i can never
plumb
      their depths

for *oniisan* never became
Oniisan.

"you no longer have a brother,"
  said
      his wife to me
    by gravesite.

it seems, a sister-in-law too
is lost to me,
as she
      no longer
  talks to me.

such is my regret   as i
give an offering
at the *Byodo-in* temple,
the
    smoke
  rises   touches
  and
      forgives

The Circle Broken

sachiko   kawai
passed   peacefully
last

week   they all do for
some
        reason
  modern medicine,
  i suppose

funny, i never
called her "Aunt"
though
            she was more
  an aunt than her sister
  Aunt sally

and i called her younger
sister   "Irene"
while she called my mother

"Auntie"

the circle drawn & tightened
as i
    inched through
  child-
        hood

her father was Grandpa
her mother
Grandma   her husband
    always the
quiet man.   Never
knew
        his first name
either—he was always
kawai-san

i called her son, Stevie,
my
    cousin, and i like
to think
he thought of me as his

In my loneliness   in
my isolation   in japan
1959,

i met
        his Hiroshima
    cousin   his   unscathed twin

the Jpze maple trees
then   swayed in the   breeze
        their morning dew
the smells and wet   of
home   i smiled

his sister, i knew as June,
a rare
        beauty

in the ugliness of
my working-class   life
  i dream of her still.

but mrs. kawai
was
        my true
    aunt

in   the early 1960s,
my mother nearly fell
with the weight of   kidney
stones

pinging and ricocheting
inside
        her abdomen   stabbing
at her with sadistic   pain

an old malady
she went to hospital
dad went to work
and i
        went
  to my aunt's

doctors operated & mom
was set to survive
                not like 1942
when
        she nearly
  died on the gurney
  in a cold Vancouver hospital
  hallway:

the
        enemy alien
of the people

so i didn't worry
[i was brave]   not
like my brother
who was told by grandma
        and aunt sally

he'd be   on the next
boat to Japan   [back in '42,

I (in '62)
    stood   naked
in the living-
room   for some reason,
hadaka   i turned away]

maybe after a morning bath,
i can still
feel

        the steam rising from
        my body   my *chinchin*
        quivering
        in the   thickly cool
        suburban   air around me.

auntie   promised me ice
cream   from their corner store
at Warden and Kingston rd.
i smiled

and   I   slept in her

bed   beside her comfortable
breathing

warming   me

i suppose i called   out
in a night-   mare   and
she took me
under   her embracing
cottonsheets

her hair suffocated
my   fear and worry

i felt *okaachan* in
the scent &
scents   of mrs. kawai.

she was
always kind to me

speaking
        with her Jpze
education   and accented
Vancouver English/
Japanese
al-
        ways   kind
always interested
in me

like auntsally, uncle eizo,
Irene
her husband Mario—
like   a gig young/

tony randall
actor   cool and smooth
chuckling   at
        stories within
    aunt sally's Coffee Time
    circle.

but the years stretch and
lengthen   and cousins
drift   a-part   the circle
elongates   snaps & shri-
vels

to-day,
        we are civil but
never as friendly
as in
        our *Japanese* childhood

we are cordial but we never
suggest grasping hands   to rejoin
redefine & shore up   the   circle

just a private family service
for *kawai-san.*

the days grow
long   [er]   as i slump
old
    [er]   and i sense
    night beginning
    to
        fall

a chill arises
in the air   of last days

and i
        look upon the
disappearing   circle
before   me
wonder-   ing

where it all went.

The Sound of Waves

the slate
          blue water
   soaked thru   his
shirt, his pants, his
under-
       wear

he took his socks off,
for some reason,
left
     them lying
on the beach

   like flat and
   rumpled   foot-
   prints in the sand

and he waded
into
     the waiting
   waters

curling black
waves   like mouths

called within   whispering
winds   recalling
lost opportunities
             lost sisters
   lost brothers   parents

lost   lovers

and he closed his eyes,
feels   the cold
       crack his legs—
his arms,
his bones   icewater
frosts the blood,
          breath—frozen
   sludge in his   lungs

and he opened his eyes
to
      withering   blind-
   ness

he left no reason, no confession   just:
shoes on his feet   and
the sound of waves
in
          the
   air.

for sam, Roy's brother

Coda to suicide

i imagine he heard jazz;
sam.
     Hey, mr. bassman,

the wild, sensual music
that last warmed

his soul.

the heaviness
              of
depression
leads
to the light of resolve.

Icestorm

(a hard rain)

black air   breathed in
   frost   and
      exhaled gelatin
  rain

  fell and hardened with
  a touch of concrete, asphalt, wood
  metal   and shingle

a surface coating of glistening glass

icy branches   turn
trees arthritic   like old men
they
     creak and groan
  in the wind

until
branches crack and collapse
to the ground.
          tree
creatures   step briefly
gingerly   unsteadily   as a cripple
before
     crumpling into

    a heap   taking down the
    wires of the modern
    age

cut off: internet, cellphone, cable,
welcome   to 1972,

yet Christmas looms.

the ice-storm   in its curtain
of snow and ice   separates isolates,
underscores
the broken bonds of family

a sister-in-law   shivers in her icebox
house   a heart of ice and frost

her son
                entertains
        his in-laws

in a distant   suburb
while the orphan uncle
wonders
                of what has been
lost;   dreams
of a time of a glacier-range of
glowing   packages
with shiny, ancient wrapping
& fancy bows   beneath the spark-
ling
bulbs of a bubble-lit   tree

of family laughing and
gathering
        around the Christ-
    mass   turkey and fixings

of jokes, stories   hopes for
the New Year

but the icestorm rages
outside   vehicles frozen
solid and stiff   wanderers and would-be
well-wishers   bundled
in layers of clothing
come to a stand   - still
against the   windstorm &
ice
     needles

while
       memories
   lie
       encased in an ironic
presence of   the absent

waiting for the sun
to   melt them

to drip
into
     streams   to flow
along the gutter   down
sewer mouths

       never
to
     return

Into the Mystic

the lazy
   lopping
  bassline

insinuates its way
into the brain
eliciting
memories feelings
emo-
   tions
that smoked in the past.

stolen moments
of
  long
 lost love

stolen by time gone in a theft
of
  an eye

yet
the flow of Top 40 music
con-tin
   -ues

and smoulders in the sleep
& ring-dust of Golden Oldies

A dream of
lying   in my brother's bed
his
        FM radio console glowing
    in the

darkness   the *Open Lid*   oozes
a
narcotic hum

Santana   plays   silky notes
under
        the glowing posters
    of the apartment

my friend's place
my
        mentor's
    home

the Revox turning
and
        whirring
blacklight images

beasts   and wind
crying
        and
    singing

hendrix burns,   morrison purrs   and
joplin rasps.

and in the mystic above,
the music
            links us
    comforts us

keeps us
from   the alien-world.

Thru' the Night

as we
     drive
  thru' the night

the darkness surrounds,
en-
    gulfing us like   animals
  trapped

in tar-oil   our mouths gulping
and gasping
       until
     we suffocate with black-lung
     congestion,

but Mike is cool
gripping   the steering wheel
of
    his late-model Oldsmobile
88   - a lucky number.

driver's
     side
window open   the breeze
makes his eyes   squint,
the cigarette   burns brightly
as he inhales
and
    then
  hangs loose from his lips
  as he exhales.

cool, yeah cool.

distant vistas are blind,
my
        mind's eye
etches   the shining
horizon   of
land-
        scapes
and endless fields

and suns rise
and set   and meld
into one   hot
                brightness

but a sadness
comes
        over me

instinctively   knowing
this
        is my REM-sleep
as the car   vibrates,
eats up the road
that
        has no whitelines   no
        guardrails   no passing
        signs
                [billboard
            or otherwise.

I look at Mike
and   can no longer
see
        him   but the music
plays on from the radio:
springsteen   bob seger
and the silver bullet band
meatloaf   by the
                    dash-
                board light

and then he's gone   in a puff
of grey smoke]

but
I know he's happy
to be   in his own combo:

Mythical Mike
and the
        Blind Vistas.

and when
        we meet again
    hurtling thru'
    the night

we will mediate before
the dark
            fields of Nirvana
and   become
part of the myth.

Long AGo

death
    fixes
  a point

and you drift away
in
    the flow
  of space & time

until you notice
that your loved ones lived
long   ago.

doesn't matter whether
it was
    mother, father, friend or
    brother

you can't feel their presence
any
      more

not like savouring the gourmet
spices and   oil of a restaurant

    that pool in the
    garlic
        of the falling dark

or like drawing the clean lines of
a landscape within the brighten-
ing sky

or like cupping a sunset
in the hands   for only a
breathing moment.

only letters, photographs,
    home movies   diaries
  [if you're lucky   ] and
  memories   remain

and then there's   that fixed point in-
between   the
when
        and then

and soon you become Long AGo

Dazzling Blue

when I a-
    woke   from
the   depths of age-less
sleep

[on the first day]

the riverstream
of
    wind   crossed
  my face

and comfort-ed   me;

when   the sound
of
    city-dust
        landed
  on my tongue

I tasted sweetness   light
and
      salt:
    nourishing me;

when I gazed skyward

I tingled to
the blue
        wispy
  clouds   &   sun

my arms rose and my
hands held   the air
in
        all its fullness
    with all its

sparkling effervescence

the dazzling
blue
        at the rise of
    day

until
        the overflow
washed over me

wetting
            my body
with wonder & well-
ness.   the thrill of the
blue

        prickled my skin
        stung my eyes
        and my being shivered.

and when I return
to   the long breathless
sleep
        [on the
very last day]

I will
     dream
of the moment
I awake
       again
and marvel   in awe

at   the dazzling blue

Epilogue

Love at #27

quiet music
reaches out in the
blackness of a
sub-
      dued house

a sad, indistinct melody
hangs
      in the leaden air,

but the notes
reach   out
like lovin'
arms   translucent
hands
     cup
   the face

she is music to me
light,
     floating,
   and free.

as we lie in bed in silence

my hand traverses
the
   cold tundra
 of sheets looking

for connection

and then I grasp her hand   beneath
soft breathing

and I squeeze
and she squeezes back   even
in her solid   sleep

      as my thoughts thin
      into fallen-sleep

i   know she'll be there
when I awake

such is love.

for tane

Glossary

Beiju	88th birthday
Byodo-in	Buddhist temple in Honolulu and Kyoto
chan-to, chan-to, chan-to	rhythmic onomatopoeic sound of music
chin chin	penis (child's term)
Dharma	Teachings of the Buddha
dombura kokko sukkokko	onomatopoeic sound of a rolling sphere
go-ro go-ro go-ro	onomatopoeic sound of falling object
hachimaki	headband
hadaka	naked
haole	white person (Hawaiian term)
in gassho	in gratitude (Buddhist term)
inemuri	the practice of dozing at school or work
Issei	pioneer generation of Japanese immigrants
kami-no ke	hair; kami also means god or paper
Kanaloa	Hawaiian god of the Underworld
Kannon	Buddhist goddess of mercy
Kansai, Kanto	Osaka/Kyoto region, Tokyo region
Kiyomzu-dera	temple in Kyoto

koshi	back
kuchi	mouth
minyo	Japanese folk song
Namu Amida Butsu	In the name of the Buddha
Nikkei	of Japanese heritage living outside of Japan
o-ame	severe rain storm
odori	Japanese folk dance
Okaa, Okaasan, Okaachan	mother
Oniisan	big brother, oldest brother
Oshogatsu	New Year's Day
Otouchan, Otousan	father
totan	corrugated iron roof (Hawaiian term)
Tsuki-ga deta deta, tsuki-ga deta oi yoi-yoi	opening line of the Tanko Bushi, the Coalminer's Song. "The moon has risen...Ah Ah."
Yaren soran soran soran soran	first line of Hokkaido fishermen's song
hai hai a dokkoisho dokkoisho	Words are shouts of encouragement to pull in the nets.
Yodobashi Ka-me-ra	Japanese camera store
Yotsuya	ancient district of Tokyo